KOBE
BRYANT

BY MARTY GITLIN

Published by ABDO Publishing Company, 8000 West 78th Street, Edina, Minnesota 55439. Copyright © 2011 by Abdo Consulting Group, Inc. International copyrights reserved in all countries. No part of this book may be reproduced in any form without written permission from the publisher. SportsZone™ is a trademark and logo of ABDO Publishing Company.

Printed in the United States of America,
North Mankato, Minnesota
112010
012011

 THIS BOOK CONTAINS AT LEAST 10% RECYCLED MATERIALS.

Editor: Matt Tustison
Copy Editor: Susan M. Freese
Interior Design and Production: Craig Hinton
Cover Design: Craig Hinton

Photo Credits: Mark J. Terrill/AP Images, cover, 3, 29; Press Association via AP Images, 4; Rusty Kennedy/AP Images, 7, 10, 16; Elise Amendola/AP Images, 8; Douglas M. Bovitt/AP Images, 12, 15; Kevork Djansezian/AP Images, 19; Michael Conroy/AP Images, 20; Paul Sancya/AP Images, 22; Matt A. Brown/AP Images, 25; Houston Chronicle, Aaron M. Sprecher/AP Images, 26

Library of Congress Cataloging-in-Publication Data
Gitlin, Marty.
  Kobe Bryant : NBA champion / by Marty Gitlin.
     p. cm. — (Playmakers)
  ISBN 978-1-61714-744-9
  1. Bryant, Kobe, 1978—Juvenile literature. 2. Basketball players—United States—Biography—Juvenile literature. 3. Los Angeles Lakers (Basketball team)—Juvenile literature. I. Title.
  GV884.B794G48 2011
  796.323092—dc22
  [B]
                                    2010046207

TABLE OF CONTENTS

Kobe Bryant

CHAPTER 1

FROM PHILLY TO ITALY AND BACK AGAIN

The three-year-old child gripped a tiny foam basketball. He stared at the San Diego Clippers basketball game on the television. The child watched closely. His father was playing for the Clippers.

The child saw his dad dribble to the basket. Then he copied his hero. He ran around the living room. He leaped high into the air and slammed the ball through a small plastic hoop. The child imagined an arena

Kobe Bryant, shown in 2010, has been an NBA star for years. Bryant's father, Joe, also played in the league.

Kobe's parents named their son after a Japanese steak. Kobe beef was the specialty at a steakhouse in King of Prussia, Pennsylvania. King of Prussia is a suburb of Philadelphia. Kobe was born in Philadelphia and spent much of his youth living in King of Prussia.

filled with cheering fans. The fans often went wild during his father's games.

That child was Kobe Bryant. One day, he would be one of the best basketball players in the National Basketball Association (NBA). His dad was Joe "Jellybean" Bryant. Joe played eight years in the NBA before playing in Italy. He became a basketball star in that European country.

Kobe was born on August 23, 1978. Joe and his wife, Pam, already had two daughters by then. The Bryants soon discovered their son was a gifted athlete. Kobe loved basketball from the start. It was a game he could play by himself.

Joe helped Kobe practice when he wasn't traveling. Joe played for the Philadelphia 76ers, the Clippers, and the Houston Rockets over the years. He had high expectations when he started playing in the NBA. But his fans became disappointed in him when he didn't become a star.

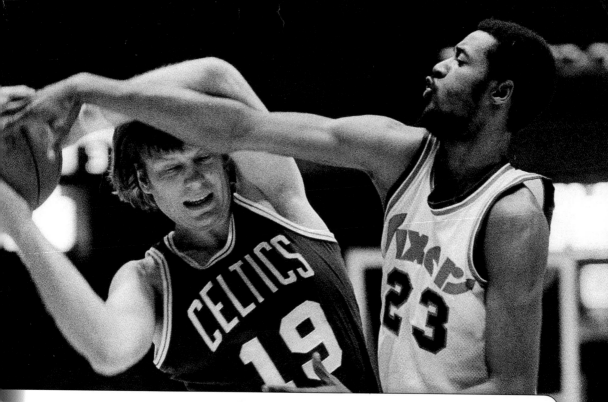

The 76ers' Joe "Jellybean" Bryant, *right*, guards the Celtics' Don Nelson in 1976. Bryant was an NBA player from 1975 to 1983.

No NBA team wanted Joe by the time he was 30 years old. So he moved his family to Italy. He played his best basketball there. He averaged 30 points per game. The Italian fans loved him!

Living in a new country was difficult for Kobe. He began first grade. But he couldn't understand the teacher or the other students. They all spoke Italian. Also, Kobe liked to play

Philadelphia's Julius Erving, *right*, shown in 1987, was an NBA
star Kobe watched when he was a youngster.

basketball. But the other children liked to play soccer. Soccer
was the most popular sport in Italy.

Living in Italy was good for Kobe in a couple of ways. He
learned to speak Italian well. He also spent a lot of time with his
parents and older sisters, Sharia and Shaya. Most nights, the
family ate dinner in their home. Then they relaxed and talked
for hours. Kobe's father didn't have to travel much.

Joe and Pam Bryant were very strict about what they let their children watch on television. They would push Kobe away when actors began kissing on the screen. When Kobe was in high school, his parents wouldn't let him watch a famous movie called *The Godfather*. They thought it was too violent.

Kobe and Joe watched videos of the top players in the NBA. Kobe studied stars such as Julius Erving and Magic Johnson. He learned every move they made with the basketball. Then he went outside and tried to copy them. He played games of one-on-one against some of his father's Italian teammates. By the time Kobe was 11 years old, he could even beat them sometimes.

Kobe was better at basketball than all the other kids. But they told him he would never be good enough to play in the NBA. They said there were too many great basketball players in the United States.

But Kobe didn't listen. He knew in his heart that he could be an NBA star. And when his family moved back to the United States in 1991, he set out to prove it.

Kobe Bryant

CHAPTER 2

GROWING INTO GREATNESS

The Bryant family moved back to the United States in 1991. They lived in the Philadelphia area. They had lived there earlier when Joe Bryant had played for the NBA's Philadelphia 76ers. Joe was from Philadelphia. Kobe was born in the city.

Kobe was now 13 years old. He was more interested in basketball than ever. He joined the well-respected Sonny Hill summer basketball league. He wrote on the application form that his future career

Kobe dunks at his high school in Pennsylvania in 1996. He was already a nationally known star.

Bryant and ex-teammate Jermaine Griffin, *right*, smile at Bryant's old high school in 2002. Coach Gregg Downer is at far left, *in tan*.

was in the NBA. One of the coaches scolded him for doing this. The coach said that only one in a million kids who dream of playing in that league actually makes it. Kobe said that he would be that kid.

People in the area started hearing about Kobe's talent. One of them was a coach at Lower Merion High School named Gregg Downer. Lower Merion was a public high school in the suburb of Ardmore. Kobe would attend the school in the fall of 1992. Downer watched Kobe play. After that, the coach stated that Kobe would definitely be in the NBA someday.

Lower Merion High School was known for its strong academic program, not its sports teams. The basketball squad was mostly average. The Aces needed a star to win some games. Kobe was the team's leading scorer as a freshman. Still, the team finished 4–17.

Kobe wanted to turn the Lower Merion Aces into a winning team. And that's just what he did as a sophomore. He led the team with 22 points and 10 rebounds per game. The Aces finished 16–6.

During Kobe's junior year, he clearly became the top high school player in Pennsylvania. He averaged 31.1 points and 10.4 rebounds per game. He helped Lower Merion win the Central League conference title.

Kobe wanted even more. He wanted the Aces to win the state championship. However, the team lost in the state tournament. Kobe had 33 points and 15 rebounds in the Aces' defeat. But he apologized to his teammates for not doing more.

Kobe was invited to play in several well-known basketball camps before his senior year in high school. He was named the Most Valuable Player (MVP) of the Keystone State Games in Pennsylvania. Kobe helped his Delaware Valley team win the title.

Kobe held back tears. He promised his teammates that he would lead them to the state crown the next year.

As a senior, Kobe was believed to be the top high school player in the United States. Kobe was offered scholarships from the top college basketball programs in the nation.

The Lower Merion Aces got off to a slow start during Kobe's final year of high school. But then Kobe helped the team win its final 27 games. The Aces made it to the state championship game. Late in that contest, they had a 45–43 lead over Erie Cathedral Prep School. Kobe grabbed a rebound and passed the ball to a teammate. The teammate scored the basket that clinched the win and the state title for the Aces. Kobe had kept his promise to his teammates. He averaged 31 points and 12 rebounds per game during his senior year.

Kobe's high school career was over. He had to decide what to do next. Would he accept a scholarship and play for

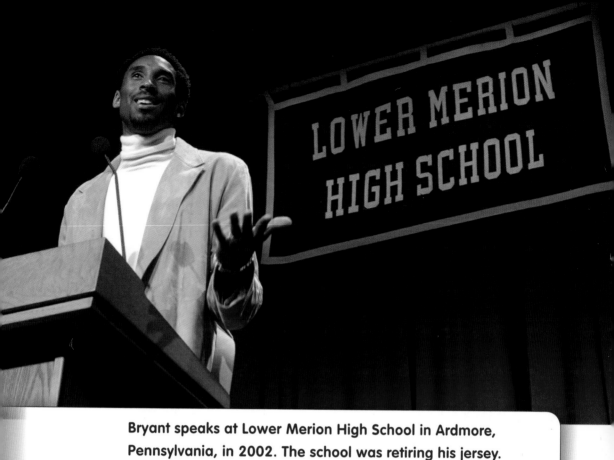

Bryant speaks at Lower Merion High School in Ardmore, Pennsylvania, in 2002. The school was retiring his jersey.

a college team? Or would he head straight to the NBA? Kobe planned to announce his decision at Lower Merion High School. Sports media from all over the country joined Kobe's friends, family, and fans to hear him announce what he was going to do.

16   **Kobe Bryant**

CHAPTER 3

ON TO NBA STARDOM

On May 6, 1996, Kobe Bryant walked up to the microphone at Lower Merion High School. He pretended that he was still thinking. Then he told the eager crowd what he had decided to do. He said he was skipping college and going straight into the NBA. His fans roared with approval! At the time, only a few players had successfully gone from high school to the NBA. Kobe believed he had the talent to do it.

In May 1996 at Lower Merion High School, Kobe announces that he is skipping college to enter the NBA.

Soon, Bryant started getting ready for the 1996 NBA Draft. He worked out with the Los Angeles Lakers. The Lakers' general manager was Jerry West. He had been one of the NBA's best players in the 1960s and 1970s. West was very impressed with Bryant. West set up a trade with the Charlotte Hornets that would bring the young star to the Lakers. The Hornets selected Bryant in the draft on June 26. Then they traded him to the Lakers for center Vlade Divac.

That summer, the Lakers also signed superstar center Shaquille O'Neal. O'Neal had been playing with the Orlando Magic. With Bryant and O'Neal, the Lakers had formed a talented duo. The Lakers hoped this pair would help them win an NBA championship.

Some people wondered whether Bryant was ready to play in the NBA. Early in his career, the answer wasn't clear. Bryant wasn't an accurate shooter. He averaged just 7.6 points per game his rookie season. But Bryant showed signs of talent. He won the slam-dunk contest during the NBA All-Star Weekend.

By the next season, Bryant was being compared to Chicago Bulls superstar Michael Jordan. Bryant played really

The Lakers' Bryant guards the Bulls' Michael Jordan in February 1998. The young Bryant was showing signs of stardom.

well in one game against the Bulls. He scored 33 points while being guarded by Jordan. Later that season, Bryant became the youngest player ever to make an NBA All-Star team.

Bryant was already a star in the eyes of the fans. But it wasn't until his fourth season, 1999–2000, that he proved he was one of basketball's greatest players. He averaged 22.5 points per game. Bryant also became known for playing well

Bryant, *left*, holds the 2002 NBA Finals title trophy and teammate Shaquille O'Neal hoists the Finals MVP Award.

under pressure. It all started in the NBA Finals that season. Even though he had a sprained ankle, Bryant scored 28 points and made the winning basket in Game 3 against the Indiana Pacers. He had 26 more points in Game 6 to help the Lakers clinch the NBA championship.

Bryant and his teammates got used to winning championships. Bryant's scoring soared to 28.5 points per

On April 18, 2001, Bryant married model Vanessa Laine. The couple had met two years earlier. They had become engaged during the 2000 playoffs. They got married the day after the 2000–01 regular season ended.

game in 2000–01. He helped the Lakers defeat his hometown Philadelphia 76ers four games to one in the NBA Finals.

In the 2002 Finals, the Lakers didn't lose even one game. Bryant averaged nearly 27 points per game in a four-game sweep of the New Jersey Nets. The Nets threatened to win Game 3. But Bryant scored 12 points in the fourth quarter to put them away. He had proven himself as one of the greatest pressure players in the NBA. He had helped the Lakers win an amazing three titles in a row. This had been done only four times in league history.

Then, in 2004, the Lakers traded O'Neal. Bryant had to prove the team could win a championship without O'Neal, the star center. That wouldn't be easy.

Kobe Bryant

CHAPTER 4

EARNING TITLES AND GIVING BACK

Kobe Bryant and Shaquille O'Neal won three NBA titles in a row with the Lakers. They had proven to be the league's best duo. Few people understood how the two stars could have trouble getting along with each other.

Their relationship became difficult after Los Angeles lost early in the 2003 playoffs. The two began arguing, and the conflict grew. Bryant and O'Neal no longer seemed like teammates.

Bryant, *front*, and Shaquille O'Neal react during the 2004 NBA Finals. Los Angeles lost to Detroit.

On January 22, 2006, Bryant scored 81 points in the Lakers' 122–104 home victory over the Toronto Raptors. This point total was the second highest ever scored in an NBA game. The only player to score more points in a game was Wilt Chamberlain of the Philadelphia Warriors. He scored 100 points in a game in March 1962.

In 2004, the Lakers played well enough to reach the NBA Finals. But the team performed poorly in the title round. Los Angeles lost in five games to the Detroit Pistons. The Lakers traded O'Neal to the Miami Heat before the next season.

Bryant wanted to prove he could win an NBA championship without O'Neal at his side. But no player can win a title alone. Bryant led the league in scoring in both the 2005–06 and 2006–07 seasons. But the Lakers didn't have enough talent as a team to reach the NBA Finals.

Then the Lakers acquired a talented 7-foot player named Pau Gasol. The team returned to the NBA Finals in 2008. But Los Angeles lost in six games to the Boston Celtics. Even though the Lakers lost, they showed they were a strong team once again. Bryant averaged 28.3 points per game. He was named the NBA's regular-season MVP for the first time.

Bryant scored a career-high 81 points, the second most in NBA history, in a January 2006 game against the Raptors.

By this time, Bryant had grown up on and off the court. He became concerned about the world around him and people less fortunate than him. After a terrible earthquake hit China in 2008, he started the Kobe Bryant China Fund. The fund donated nearly $1 million to help children in that country. In all, Bryant's organization raised more than $6 million to help Chinese children recover from the quake.

Bryant and Rayshawn Bright, age 7, visit during a 2005 charity game for those affected by Hurricane Katrina.

Bryant would also become involved in other charities. He accepted a position as the "National Celebrity Ambassador" for the After School All-Stars. The charity provides after-school programs for 72,000 low-income, inner-city kids. In addition, Bryant got involved in the Cathy's Kids Foundation. The foundation helps underprivileged youth in the Los Angeles and New York inner cities.

By the start of the 2008–09 season, many of the people who followed basketball didn't think Bryant was the NBA's top player anymore. They felt that young stars such as LeBron James were better. This idea wouldn't be put to rest until the Lakers won another NBA title. So in the 2009 playoffs, Bryant set out to prove he was still the best. He was determined to lead the Lakers to a championship.

And that's just what he did. During the regular season, he guided the Lakers to a 65–17 record. Los Angeles advanced in the postseason to face the Orlando Magic in the NBA Finals. The Lakers won four games to one to capture the title. Bryant averaged 32.4 points and 7.4 assists in the series.

Bryant was selected as the Finals MVP. It was the first time he had received this honor. O'Neal had won all the MVP Awards when the Lakers claimed three straight titles from 2000 to 2002. Bryant was thrilled to win an NBA title without O'Neal. He said, "I think we as a team answered the call because they understood the challenge that I had, and we all embraced it."

With this championship, Bryant had won four NBA titles. But he wanted another one. The Lakers finished 57–25 in the

Bryant was selected to play in every NBA All-Star Game from 1998 to 2010. He missed the game in 2010 because of an ankle injury. He won the All-Star Game MVP Award in 2002, 2007, and 2009. He shared the MVP Award in 2009 with ex-teammate Shaquille O'Neal.

2009–10 regular season. They had the best record in the NBA's Western Conference. Bryant averaged 27.0 points per game.

Los Angeles beat three playoff opponents to set up a rematch of the 2008 NBA Finals. The Lakers would play the Celtics, their longtime rivals. Bryant's shooting was off during the series. So he knew he had to help in other ways. He averaged eight rebounds per game in the series. And in Game 7, he had 15 rebounds in addition to scoring 23 points. He led the Lakers to an 83–79 home victory. This win clinched the team's second title in a row. Bryant was once again selected as the Finals MVP.

The Lakers had beaten the Celtics in a Game 7 for the first time. They had lost Game 7 to the Celtics in four earlier championship series. After winning this game, Bryant said, "This one is by far the sweetest, because it's them. This was the

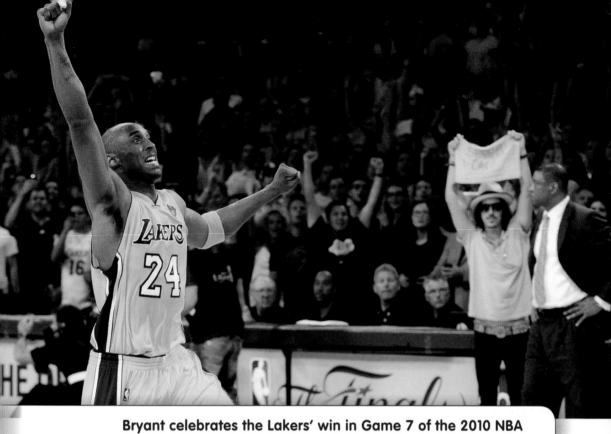

Bryant celebrates the Lakers' win in Game 7 of the 2010 NBA Finals. Los Angeles captured a second title in a row.

hardest one by far. I wanted it so bad, and sometimes when you want it so bad, it slips away from you. My guys picked me up."

Bryant clearly enjoyed winning this championship. But he didn't claim to be the greatest player in the NBA. Instead, he thanked his teammates for playing their best when the team needed it the most. Bryant showed everyone that he was a true champion on and off the court.

FUN FACTS AND QUOTES

- The feud between Kobe Bryant and Shaquille O'Neal was clearly over by the 2009 NBA All-Star Game. The former teammates played well with each other. They also shared the MVP Award. And they even shared a hug.

- Bryant has two young daughters, Natalia and Gianna. He showed his love for them after leading the Lakers to the 2010 NBA title. He held both girls in his arms as he answered questions from the media.

- "I know every series the Lakers have played in, and I know every Celtics series. I know every statistic. It meant the world to me."
  —Bryant, after Los Angeles beat Boston in seven games in the 2010 NBA Finals. The Lakers improved to 3–9 against the Celtics in Finals series.

- Bryant was unhappy with the Lakers in 2007. The team wasn't nearly as successful as it had been early in Bryant's career. Bryant was so unhappy that he asked to be traded at one point. He stayed with the team, however. The Lakers improved with the help of his leadership. In 2010, Bryant signed a contract and agreed to stay with the Lakers until at least until 2013.

WEB LINKS

To learn more about Kobe Bryant, visit ABDO Publishing Company online at **www.abdopublishing.com**. Web sites about Bryant are featured on our Book Links page. These links are routinely monitored and updated to provide the most current information available.

GLOSSARY

assist

In basketball, when one player passes the ball to another player, who then scores a basket; the player who passes the ball makes an assist.

athlete

A person who competes in a sport.

charity

Money given or work done to help people in need.

draft

In the NBA, an event held each June in which the teams take turns selecting from among the top college and international players.

league

In sports, a group of teams that play against each other. Professional basketball teams are part of the National Basketball Association (NBA). The NBA is divided into the Western Conference and the Eastern Conference.

media

Organizations that provide information to the public, such as newspapers and magazines, radio and television, and the Internet.

NBA

The National Basketball Association. As of 2010, the NBA had 30 teams based in cities across the United States and Canada.

NBA All-Star Game

A game played every year in February in which the best NBA players from the Eastern Conference play against the best players from the Western Conference.

rebound

In basketball, to grab the ball after a missed shot.

scholarship

Money for tuition and other expenses provided by a college or other organization to a student, such as a top high school athlete.

INDEX

FURTHER RESOURCES

Heisler, Mark. *Kobe and the New Lakers' Dynasty*. Chicago: Triumph Books, 2009.

Los Angeles Times. *The Los Angeles Lakers: 50 Amazing Years in the City of Angels (revised and expanded edition)*. N.p.: Time Capsule Press, LLC, 2010.

Simmons, Bill. *The Book of Basketball: The NBA According to the Sports Guy*. New York: Random House, 2009.